TEACHING
THE BIBLE
TO ELEMENTARY
CHILDREN

REVISED EDITION

DICK MURRAY

Assisted by Ruth Murray Alexander
and Ellen Shepard

DISCIPLESHIP RESOURCES

P.O. BOX 840 • NASHVILLE,TN 37202-0840

To my childhood Sunday school teachers
at First United Methodist Church, Des Moines, Iowa,
1925–1936:

EDITH MCBETH, JEANETTE PICKFORD,
MADGE KUSSART, MR. HARDER, ETHEL MCCLELLAN,
and others whose names I don't recall

Images © 1997 PhotoDisc, Inc.

ISBN: 0-88177-222-4

Revised Edition

DR222

CONTENTS

THROUGH BIBLE STUDY

THE CHURCH SEEKS

TO HELP CHILDREN

BECOME INCREASINGLY AWARE

OF GOD'S SEEKING LOVE

AS KNOWN ESPECIALLY

IN JESUS CHRIST THAT THEY

MAY RESPOND IN FAITH

AND IN LOVE.

SOME DO'S FOR TEACHING THE BIBLE TO CHILDREN

1. Make teaching the Bible to children a priority in your church.

2. Make learning the Scriptures a priority for children both in Sunday school and in other educational settings. Include a variety of group activities that encourage (but that do not coerce) memorizing key Scripture verses and stories.

3. Offer teachers and parents training events for learning how to tell Bible stories to children and for practicing storytelling. (See Chapter 5.)

4. Encourage parents to help children learn Scripture by sending home curriculum activity sheets and/or photocopied portions of Scripture with instructions for parents to follow.

5. Urge the pastor to include Bible stories—told so that they can be understood by children—in Sunday morning congregational worship.

6. Help children follow along in their own Bibles or in pew Bibles as Scripture lessons are read during congregational worship.

7. Do all teaching of Scripture in a loving way. Remember, we study the Bible to know God, not simply to know the Bible. God is love, and we and our children help each other learn about and experience that love as we study the Bible together.

8. Approach both children and the Bible with joy.

TEACHING FOR FAITH DEVELOPMENT AND DISCIPLESHIP

CHILDREN UNDERSTAND AS CHILDREN

Which came first, the Bible or the church? This question does not have an easy answer. On the one hand, we know that the diverse content of the Bible was brought together by the church of the first, second, and third centuries. The early church used divine inspiration and probable authorship as basic criteria and decided the arrangement of the books, what to put in, and what to leave out.

On the other hand, the content of the Old Testament and much of the New Testament existed in both oral and written forms before the church decided it was to be the content of the Bible and before the church itself developed. So which came first, the Bible or the church?

How we answer the question is not as important as our recognition that the Bible, indeed, is the church's book. In one form or another the church has heard in the Bible the Word of God.

Because we believe that God's word comes to us through the pages of the Bible, we want our children to both read and hear that word. Yet the Bible is an adult book. Written by adults for adults, the Bible contains poetry, history, drama, and prose that are impossible for children to understand in the same way that adults do. Nevertheless, from earliest biblical times adults have felt led to teach their children key passages and stories from the Bible. Their purpose and ours is not that children simply be able to know or quote the Bible but that children come to know and love God as revealed through the Bible's verses and stories.

In the book *The Bible: A Child's Playground*, Roger and Gertrude Gobbell suggest: "Let the Bible be the Bible. Let children be children." These statements are the key to using the Bible with children. We must not try to make the Bible what it isn't so that children can better understand the adult concepts. Neither do we dare try to force children to understand the Bible as an adult would. Children understand the Bible as children understand.

Then how *do* we teach children the Bible? Here's a clue. Do you remember when as a young child you learned the following fingerplay?

> *Here is the church;*
> *Here is the steeple.*
> *Open the doors*
> *And see all the people.*

You probably learned to fold your hands so that your fingers were hidden inside. As soon as you opened your hands, you revealed "the people"—your fingers. You wiggled your fingers to show that in the church people are *active* and *involved*.

An active and involved church includes active and involved children. Active and involved children learn best through active and involved learning techniques—techniques that allow for use of all their senses. Children can sit and listen to adult teachers briefly and will be interested and responsive (especially younger children) when the teacher tells a story well; but for the Bible to come alive for children, they need to be involved with more than their ears alone most of the time.

WHO ARE ELEMENTARY CHILDREN?

As experienced teachers and parents know, elementary children are not all that elementary. *Elementary* means simple or basic, but the elementary children I know and have observed are complex individuals motivated or held back by a wide range of cultural and genetic factors. Their individual behavior has many roots, some apparent and many hidden. Entering first grade at about six years of age and completing sixth grade at about twelve, our elementary children are a wonderful gift and challenge to us.

GROUPING ELEMENTARY CHILDREN

Some churches have only two or three children, sometimes from the same family (in which case they are used to working—and quarreling—together). In such churches children of various ages, both preschool and elementary children, are usually placed together in one class to work together on some activities and alone on others.

Many other churches with small numbers of children divide them into two classes based on their reading ability. Those who read (usually all the elementary children) are separated from those who do not yet have that skill (usually all the preschool children), and each group has a teacher.

Many churches with large numbers of children provide elementary children with a separate class or classes for each school grade—first through sixth. Each class may have two or more teachers.

Because curriculum resources for elementary children are often developed to serve two-grade groupings—first and second, third and fourth, and fifth and sixth grades—churches who have moderate numbers of children in each grade find having three elementary classes, each with one or two teachers, convenient. Every congregation chooses the grouping that best suits the children and teachers it has available.

This book takes a middle ground and deals with *younger elementary* children (first, second, and third graders) and *older elementary* children (fourth, fifth, and sixth graders). The difference in the maturity of skills between the third and fourth grades serves as a functional division.

TEACHING YOUNGER ELEMENTARY CHILDREN

Some children enter the first grade from a stimulating home environment and a strong kindergarten experience. Other children have had neither, so they need a great deal of special attention and help. Most first and second graders have beginning reading skills and approach reading with considerable excitement. The excitement stems from the mind-blowing experience of being able to identify many words and to put them together in interesting sentences either on the written page or on the computer screen. The Bible and Bible stories provide arenas for these children to practice their newly learned reading skills.

Younger elementary children, especially at seven or eight, tend to have less interest in the stories than in asking the questions, Is it true? Did that *really* happen? Did Jesus actually do that? How do you know? When met with tough questions, we adults must remember what was said earlier: "Let the Bible be the Bible. Let children be children." We should not feel that we have to explain all the mystery. We should keep our responses as honest and open-ended as possible so that children can be nurtured by a growing understanding as they grow older. It is perfectly all right to say, "We don't know," or to ask, "What do you think?" Inviting children to reflect on what they think helps them claim as their own the story they have read or heard.

Remember that children this age are active, messy learners. Their encounters with the Bible stories need to be reinforced with activities that allow them to use all of their senses. Their learning can be enhanced by acting out the Bible story, crafting a sheep like the one the shepherd searched for, painting the manger scene, learning actions to a song based on the Bible story, learning selected words from the key verse in American Sign Language, eating a snack of Bible-times foods, and so forth.

TEACHING OLDER ELEMENTARY CHILDREN

Children in the fourth, fifth, and sixth grades are preadolescents who are increasingly aware of themselves. These children are often self-confident but can also be self-conscious and shy around adults. Boy-girl competition is often enjoyed at this age, and the children are proud of acknowledged accomplishments.

We traditionally give Bibles to third or fourth graders. Then we expect them quickly to learn their way around in the Bible, the names of the books, and how to find references. They need to be taught to distinguish between the Old Testament and the New Testament, what is meant by books of the Bible, how books are arranged in chapters and verses, and how to write references.

We can encourage older elementary children to look things up for themselves, to check out facts in references such as Bible dictionaries and atlases, and to compare different translations and paraphrases. For these children our role as teacher is to be a guide who suggests sources of information rather than a provider of the information. Once again a variety of activities is important.

In addition to telling a Bible story, we can provide opportunities for the boys and girls to read the story from their own Bibles. They can read in silence or aloud in unison. Sometimes good readers eagerly volunteer to read to the group and can be encouraged to do so. We must *never* embarrass poor readers or those who stutter by asking everyone to read around the circle or by calling on children who habitually do badly. Some older elementary children are still struggling to read. They are helped far more if they read in a group than if they are forced to read badly by themselves.

Every elementary classroom needs enough Bibles of the same translation for each child to use one in class. These Bibles can reside on a shelf in the children's room or in a study space in the church. Right beside the Bibles (not in the church library or in some other room down the hall) should be lodged one or more references such as a Bible dictionary, a Bible atlas, a Bible concordance, and Gospel parallels.

If money for purchasing these resources is an issue for you, appeal to the congregation for funds. What better cause could someone adopt than making available Bibles and Bible helps for the children to use? Let's provide our children with the resources they need.

CHILDREN AND FAITH

Faith is always a gift of God. We do not teach faith to our children, nor do we give faith to our children. We often wish we could do one or the other, but we cannot. Nevertheless, our children can have as full a faith while they are still children as we adults have; that faith is simply different.

John Westerhoff III has been a leader in helping us understand the faith of elementary children. In his book *Will Our Children Have Faith?* Westerhoff describes the faith of young children in terms of "experienced faith" and "affiliative faith" (Seabury, 1976; pages 91–96).

EXPERIENCED FAITH

Pre-elementary children and younger elementary children do not choose their faith, nor do they *intellectually understand* their faith. But they do experience the faith as practiced by their parents and others around them. They *experience* trust, love, and acceptance and intuitively share in Christian faith at their own level of understanding.

It is important for us to understand that the faith of our children is *real* faith. Children seem to have a natural openness to the experience of the love of God, as they do to the experience of the love of parents. Children both give and receive that love. When Jesus said that adults must become as little children, he must have been referring, at least in part, to this natural openness to the love of God—called faith.

AFFILIATIVE FAITH

Westerhoff uses this term to describe the faith of older children, who want to affiliate with—to become a part of—the faith they have, up to this point, simply experienced. Important to affiliative faith is a sense of belonging to and identifying with the faith community. At ages eleven and twelve children accept as their own the traditions, affirmations, and practices of the faith they have been experiencing. At this age children's decisions are not intellectually informed, individual decisions. They are I-want-to-be-a-part decisions; and they are valid faith decisions.

Westerhoff points out that a child's faith is like a tree. When the tree is young, it is thin and short; but the sapling is nevertheless a full and complete tree. Years later the tree will have added many growth rings and will have grown much taller, but it will never be a more complete tree than it was when it was young (*Will Our Children Have Faith?; pages 89–91*).

In the church community a primary goal is to nurture children for growth in the faith even as a young tree is nurtured for growth. How can teachers and parents teach so that knowledge of the Bible and involvement with the Bible contribute to children's faith development?

CHILDREN LEARNING

I grew up in Iowa, a state that had consolidated schools quite early. Children often spent a large part of an hour on the school bus. A common saying was, "It's too bad when the bus gets to school. That's when the learning stops and the education begins."

What do children learn on a school bus? They learn the *really* important things in life, such as how to deal with a bully, how to attract the opposite sex, and how to express one's ideas and feelings. This kind of learning is what I call basic learning.

The saying did not mean that in Iowa children did not learn much in school. The point of the saying is that important learning, basic learning, goes on all the time, not only in school. Planned, structured learning is only a small part of the whole of children's learning. Children learn by

✔ being motivated, interested, and involved;

✔ imitating;

✔ listening and then trying out what they hear;

✔ repeating, doing or saying something over and over;

✔ making sense of things they hear or see even though their understanding of those things will change over the years.

What is true of other learning is also true, of course, of Christian education; it does not take place only at church or in Sunday school. Many people have said that hardly anything can be expected to be accomplished in the one hour or less per week that children spend in Sunday school. The truth is that an hour in Sunday school is far from our entire opportunity to teach about faith and discipleship. All of us learn about and have opportunities to grow in faith and discipleship all the time.

Children learn discipleship at home and from all of their church experience. They learn from their experiences with adults and with one another. They learn on the way to church in the car. They learn on the playground.

Children learn about faith and discipleship from family members in the home. We have formal and informal rituals by which children learn. A fine example of a ritual that helps Jewish children learn about their faith is the traditional Seder meal at Passover time. The youngest child is taught to ask four questions to which the father is to reply with answers based on the description of the Passover event in Exodus 12. The questions are

"Why is this night different from all other nights? For on all other nights we eat either leavened bread or unleavened, but on this night only unleavened."

"Why on this night do we eat bitter herbs?"

"Why do we dip the herbs twice?"

"Why on this night do we recline when we eat?"

The formality of the ritual gives both the parents and the children a structure within which they can discuss an important event in their history and faith. Similar rituals in Christian homes include the use of Advent wreaths and devotionals, Lenten giving practices, and studies such as FaithHome (Abingdon, 1997) that encourage parents and children to read Scripture and to talk together about their beliefs.

We teach the Bible to elementary children not just so that they will know the Bible itself but so that they will know God, especially as God can be known through Jesus Christ. We teach what prominent Christian educator and writer Dorothy Jean Furnish describes as the "For-us-ness" of God. Thus, above all else, the *seeking* love of God is at the center of our teaching the Bible.

POINTS TO REMEMBER

✔ Children become Christian by meeting Jesus Christ in the Christian community: the church and the family.

✔ This community depends upon the Bible to reveal God and Jesus Christ.

✔ The church uses the Bible in all that it does—its worship, its teaching, its service.

✔ The Bible is the center point of the church's memory, and children must share in that memory if they are to be Christian.

✔ Although the Bible was written for adults, children can learn the key truths of the Bible and can feel their way into its stories.

✔ The faith of children is a full and real faith equal to their needs. Nevertheless, the way they express it and act it out is largely based on how they see it modeled in adults.

✔ Children add to their knowledge of the Bible and develop more mature faith year by year as they participate in the ministries of the church.

✔ Children learn by involvement and active participation, which both motivate them and enable them to make ideas their own.

2 THE ART OF TELLING BIBLE STORIES

If there were no stories in the world,
people would die of seriousness.
—AN ELEMENTARY CHILD

SAME STORY—DIFFERENT MEANINGS

Children of different ages like stories of different kinds. They also hear, share, and become involved in stories in different ways. Let's compare the story of God speaking to Moses on the mountain as told to younger elementary children and as told to older elementary children.

A teacher of first and second graders (ages six and seven) is telling the story. She smiles and says:

Do you remember last week's story about a man named Moses? Can you say *Moses?* Let's say it again. *Moses.*

Moses was a Hebrew. You remember that Hebrews worshiped God. God loved the Hebrews, and the Hebrews loved God.

One hot, sunny day Moses was taking care of sheep out on a rocky mountainside. Moses was hot and tired, so he sat down to rest. Suddenly Moses heard something. It sounded like a voice was calling his name: "Moses! Moses!"

Moses was puzzled, but he said, "Here I am." Then Moses realized that the voice was God's voice.

God said, "Take off your sandals because you are standing on holy ground. I am the God of your ancestors."

Moses hid his face because he was afraid to look at God.

Then God said, "Moses, I have a job for you. I want you to go to Egypt and free the Hebrew people from Pharaoh."

Moses replied, "God, you have to be kidding. I'm the wrong person. I can't do that!"

But, girls and boys, do you know what happened? Moses did as God told him, and God was with Moses all the way.

Isn't that an interesting story? Have you heard that story before? Look at this picture. What does Moses have in his hand? A stick? Do you remember what it is called? A crook. Do you know what shepherds do with a crook?

I wonder how Moses felt. Who would like to play Moses? Put on this headdress and tell us what happened. Who wants to be a sheep?

(Elementary classes enjoy acting out Bible stories. While costumes are not necessary, a box of colorful headdresses is useful to help the children get into the spirit of the story. Hemmed 24-inch-by-36-inch pieces of material and 24-inch-long headbands to tie around the head make great headdresses.)

Why is the teacher telling first and second graders this story? Why is she involving them in thinking and feeling about this story? Does she think that they will remember the story? Does she believe that their knowing the story will have an important influence on their lives?

This teacher is telling a story that is a part of *the* story, the story of God making Godself known to humankind. This story tells of a people who came to believe that *God is for us.* They came to believe that when we ignore or disobey God, God does not give up on us. This God keeps loving us no matter what.

The teacher is telling children the story of Moses' hearing God and is enouraging them to respond to the story because she wants the church's story to become the children's story. She wants them to remember it, to feel it, and to know that we value this important story.

MOSES AND OLDER ELEMENTARY CHILDREN

Once again the story is of God speaking to Moses on the mountain, but the children are in the fifth and sixth grades. They are ten, eleven, and possibly twelve.

They want *to know*!

How could Moses hear God? Why was the bush not burning? Where was Midian? Where was Egypt in relation to Midian?

The teacher tells parts of the story but also leads the class in reading from Exodus 3:1-12 as a group. As the class reads in unison, the teacher sees that some children are reading easily, others are having difficulty, and some are hardly reading at all. Some children know most of the words, but others seem to struggle over every phrase. But no child is *embarrassed,* because no one is reading alone; the poor readers are hidden in the group. The teacher praises the group reading while helping occasionally with the pronunciation of difficult words.

When the reading is concluded, the teacher reviews the story by asking questions. To help the children remember the story correctly, she asks about facts such as what country Moses was in when he heard God (Midian). To help girls and boys get into the story, she asks, "How do you think Moses felt? How would you have felt?" She is not critical of answers to the feeling-level questions because she knows that there are no correct answers to questions of this sort. (Remember: "Let the Bible be the Bible. Let children be children.")

The teacher brings out a map that includes Egypt, Sinai, Midian, and Palestine. She asks the class to identify various places and helps the children do so. Each child is encouraged but not required to draw her or his own map.

"What do we know about Midian?" the teacher asks. Some of the boys and girls look up *Midian,* using a Bible dictionary or a Bible atlas that is kept in the room. With the teacher's help, they read and report to the class. (See Chapter 4.)

The key to holding the interest of older elementary children is letting them do the work themselves. A good teacher keeps them involved.

STORYTELLERS ARE NOT ALL THE SAME

Each of us is different. We tell stories differently and in different circumstances.

Many churches have a children's time during the worship service on Sunday morning. In some churches the children are invited to come to the chancel for what is sometimes called a children's sermon. Other churches have the boys and girls simply remain with their parents in the pews. Often during children's time the pastor or another person tells a Bible story to the children. The children who are present represent a wide age range, but the majority often are preschoolers and younger elementary children.

Here is a story that has been told during children's time at St. Luke United Methodist Church in Houston, Texas. The storyteller is Ellen Shepard, a church staff member.

Jesus told many stories in the Bible. Do you remember the story about a shepherd who had exactly one hundred sheep? Now, one hundred is a lot of sheep; but this shepherd knew his sheep the same way our parents and grandparents know us. He could tell which sheep he was looking at by the shape of its back, the way it walked, even the way it held its head.

Every night the shepherd counted his sheep. Every night he counted exactly one hundred sheep.

One night the shepherd was very tired. He and the sheep had gone a long way to a new place that day. He started counting the sheep. He counted only ninety-nine sheep— not one hundred. He counted again. Only ninety-nine. The shepherd was worried; a lump came into his throat. One of the sheep was missing.

It took the shepherd only a moment to decide what to do. He had to look for the sheep that wasn't there. He knew exactly which one was missing.

He went back the way he had been that day. He looked everywhere. He climbed the hills and went through rough bushes. He slipped on rocks. He called for the sheep. He listened. He walked farther. He kept wandering, searching, calling, and listening.

Finally . . . he heard a faint noise. What was it? Could it be the sheep? Then he realized that the noise was a *b-a-a-a*. It *was* the sheep!

The shepherd ran to the sheep and picked it up. He put it on his shoulders so that he could carry it back to the other sheep. The shepherd was tired. The sheep was tired. But The shepherd was very happy that he had found the lost sheep. (Adapted from Luke 15:3-6.)

What has Ellen done to the story? First, she has not *added* any-one to the story. For example, she has not injected a modern-day child into the story to help children feel that they are there. She has let the Bible be the Bible.

Then she has used her imagination to enhance the setting. She has added emotions that are consistent with emotions that a shepherd might feel in the situation.

She has also let the children be children. Jesus told this story to illustrate God's rejoicing over the recovery of a person who has gone astray, likening God to a shepherd and the person to a sheep. This kind of abstraction is just beginning to be understood by older elementary children. It would be lost on the children who make up most of Ellen's audience.

In a classroom of fifth and sixth grade children, we would properly ask, "Why do you think Jesus told the story? What did Jesus want us to know?" The answer is that Jesus wanted his audience to know that God is persistently seeking to make God's love known to all people under all conditions and that *every* person counts individually.

USING ALL OUR SENSES IN STORYTELLING

One good way to help children imagine their way into a Bible story is to ask them to use *all* their senses—not just hearing but also seeing, smelling, touching, and tasting. After all, God has given each of us eyes to see, ears to hear, noses to smell, mouths to taste, and skin to feel.

For example, imagine that you are telling the story of Jesus' preaching from the boat in Matthew 13:1-3. At first Jesus is sitting beside the sea. But so many people are in the crowd that Jesus gets into a boat. The people are standing on the beach. Sitting in the boat, Jesus continues speaking to the people.

Ask the children to imagine that each of them is one of the Hebrew children who were there. *What can they see?* They may see the water, the rocking boat, and other boats farther out in the lake.

What can they smell? They may smell fish, water, people, and maybe some animals.

What can they hear? They may hear Jesus speaking, the boat creaking, and the water lapping against the boat.

What might Jesus be saying? Lead the children in remembering teachings of Jesus at various other times during his ministry—for example, commandments such as Love your neighbor as yourself.

What can they feel? Can they feel the breeze coming off the lake? Can they feel the pressure of the crowd?

Ask the children how they feel imagining that they are there. Give them plenty of time for discussion.

Follow up with activities that allow the children to use all of their senses. Let them create an audiotape of the sounds that might have been heard. Enjoy a snack of tuna and crackers, letting them smell the fish and remember the story. Ask them to draw a picture of the scene from the boat or to write a litany expressing feelings elicited by the story. Let them construct a model boat from balsa wood and float it on water.

TELLING THE STORY

The stories in the Old Testament are the stories Jesus learned as a child. The stories in the New Testament are either stories Jesus told or stories about Jesus and his disciples. All of these stories have value. Nevertheless, it is more important for children (and for us as well) to know the key stories well than to have heard many stories only one time.

The ancient skill of storytelling is the teacher's most powerful tool. We need to learn the stories and to tell them to children in our own words with emotion and emphasis. We must let our bodies gesture the words. If we let our eyes dance as we speak of Jesus' eyes, we will see the children's eyes dance as well.

We should *never add* persons to Bible stories who could not possibly have been there. For example, including modern children in biblical stories is confusing to children and *is simply false*. Doing so is a distortion of the Bible story.

We can help children claim the stories as their own by allowing them to retell the stories they have heard. We can encourage group telling of stories, asking individuals to contribute details; we can start a familiar story, then let the children complete its telling, helping them refer to the Bible to see if their memory is accurate.

As they hear, and participate in telling, stories from the Bible, elementary children share in the Christian faith at their own level of understanding. The stories will stay with them as they grow and that level of understanding changes.

POINTS TO REMEMBER

✔ Hearing a story once is not sufficient if we believe that the story is worth remembering.

✔ Children love stories that they have heard repeatedly and that they can tell in their own words.

✔ A story heard over and over becomes the child's story because the child remembers the details better than the adult does.

✔ It is important to tell the story of Jesus and his love over and over until it becomes "my" story for both teacher and child.

✔ Stories help children share in our joint memory as the children remember what we value in our lives.

MEMORIZING: BY PARTICIPATION, FOR PARTICIPATION

3

When Martin, my grandson, was three years old, I began teaching him the Gloria Patri as I drove him around in my car. While I sang, "Glory be to the Father," Martin was singing, "Glory Papa—Glory Papa." A few weeks later we were sitting together in a worship service. As we began singing the Gloria, Martin tugged on my pants leg and said, "They are singing our song, Pa-Pa. They are singing our song!"

Wow—that is what Christian teaching and learning is all about. We want the worship service and the Bible to become "ours" to our children. Although not yet of elementary age, Martin was learning by participation for greater participation. Through frequent repetition, the Gloria Patri was becoming his.

One time when he was about four, I asked Martin to tell me the words to a hymn his children's choir was to sing. He said, "I don't know the words except when I'm singing with everyone else; then I know them." That kind of knowing is the knowledge we seek for our children in using group participation.

Who of us *really* understands the Gloria? The collection of symbolic words has been used by the church for centuries to symbolize the unity of the Old and New Testaments. Over the years Martin will come to broader and deeper understanding of this regular part of most worship services, as will his grandfather. Learning portions of the Bible such as Matthew 6:9-13 will lead children to the same kind of gradual understanding.

REPETITION: THE WAY WE LEARN

In these few verses of the sixth chapter of the Gospel of Matthew are the words for the prayer used most by most Christians—the Lord's Prayer. Most Christians include an ending added by the early church, and many Christians differ over the use of the words *debts, trespasses,* and *sins;* but we teach our children to say whatever words we use regularly in our worship.

When we teach the Bible to children, this prayer is one of the most important portions of the Bible we want them to learn. *Why?* It is the prayer that Jesus said should be the model for prayer. The Lord's Prayer is the universal prayer of Christians and is used in every public worship service in many churches.

How does a child learn Matthew 6:9-15—the Lord's Prayer? Children learn this prayer by saying it themselves and by participating with others as others say it. Children say the prayer over and over—in worship, at home as grace, in Sunday school, and in play.

I once visited a first grade Sunday school class of six-year-olds on the third Sunday of Advent. The lesson focused on a story about Jesus. On the wall, not very high, where six-year-old persons could easily read it, was a large poster that read *OUR FATHER WHO ART IN HEAVEN . . . .*

The poster had been in the same spot on that wall for the previous three months. For eleven consecutive Sundays that class had gathered in front of the poster and nine children and two teachers had held hands, looked at the words, and prayed the Lord's Prayer. Most of the children could not yet read many of the words.

Many of those children attended congregational worship most Sundays. In the worship service those children also prayed the Lord's Prayer with their parents and the congregation.

At the suggestion of their teachers, some of those children and their parents also used this passage as a prayer of thanks at some of their meals. By saying the words over and over in a variety of settings, the children began to feel at home with this part of the Bible.

Did those six-year-olds know the Lord's Prayer? The answers to that question are yes and no.

They knew the prayer in that they were able to say the words along with others. Also, they recognized it as an important prayer for Christians; therefore the prayer became important for many of them. Most of those boys and girls have continued to recall words and phrases from this prayer and will do so for the rest of their lives. At six they knew this prayer well enough that they could take part with adults in praying it.

We would have to say, however, that in some ways those six-year-olds did not "know" the prayer. For instance, only a few of those children could say the words of this prayer by themselves without mistakes. And none of those children understood what "Your kingdom come" means (in many ways, of course, neither do we). Nevertheless, through repetition these words were being engraved on their minds.

Another early experience I had with my grandson demonstrates a way young children learn. Again during a worship service, we were praying the Lord's Prayer. I opened my eyes and saw that Martin's eyes were fixed on my lips. He was saying the words as he watched me say the words. As I closed my eyes again, I was conscious that my example was being followed. Neither of us ever mentioned the incident later, and I'm sure Martin was not really aware that it had occurred.

What is going on in the kind of memorization that both the six-year-olds and Martin participated in? I call it memorization *by* participation *for* participation.

Children want to participate. Children want to know how to participate. Thus, children *want to know*.

When children learn to count 1, 2, 3, 4, they are allowed by that knowledge to participate in arithmetic. When children learn to identify the letters A, B, C, and D, they have made a beginning that will allow them to participate in reading and writing—in written communication.

When children learn Matthew, Mark, Luke, and John, that knowledge is one aspect that will allow them to participate in Bible study. When children learn the Lord's Prayer (Matthew 6:9-13), they are able to participate in the worship service.

All children like to *know*. All children want to participate. Memorization *by participation* enables a child to participate more.

MEMORIZATION WITHOUT INTIMIDATION

In the past, much memorization was done by individual recitation. A child was believed to know something when she or he could stand up and say it without help. Some children can do so readily and easily. However, some children do so only with considerable effort; and other children cannot do so at all.

Individual recitation does motivate some children to do well, but it humiliates other children. For the latter, individual recitation is often a cause for feeling bad about themselves. They may want to stay away from Sunday school in order to avoid having to recite.

Memorization by participation concentrates on seeing, hearing, writing, and saying something in a variety of ways, usually in a group. To encourage meaningful memorization, we use good humor, fun, and love. When learning Scripture is fun, children will continue learning Scripture beyond the classroom. We need to relax and remember that the success of teaching is not judged by the student's ability to recite Scripture. The success of teaching comes from instilling a love of learning.

Memorizing by participation, for participation, implies working with a group over a period of time. In order to learn a passage in this way children need to

✔ Hear it said—many times;
✔ Say it in a group—many times;
✔ Look at the words on the wall and be led to say the words while looking at them;
✔ Help a slower child read and say the words better;
✔ Read the words in the Bible;
✔ Write the words in a notebook;
✔ Sing the words in Sunday school songs and in the hymns of the church;
✔ Play games of word matching and recall;
✔ Create works of art that include the words of the passage.

Does a child know something better if she or he can stand up and say it alone than if he or she has heard, seen, and said it in a group thirty times over a four-month period? Over the long run, I doubt that individual recitation makes a child know a passage better. However, the *attitude* of both teacher and pupil can have a large role in either process.

We learn love by being loved and by loving ourselves. A child learns the love of God, in part, through experiencing our love. Being sensitive to a child's feelings shows our love for the child.

WHAT ABOUT PARENTS?

Many parents welcome and are enthusiastic about a plan for biblical memorization. They discover that they receive personal benefit from the church's request that they help their children memorize portions of the Bible. In working with their children, they have an opportunity to discuss Christian beliefs and to deal with questions their children raise concerning meanings. Sometimes their children's enthusiasm prompts parents to want to know more for themselves.

Parental support is of great importance. However, we need to stress that their support is most helpful when it is warm, caring, and loving. Parents are most supportive when the child knows that he or she is loved regardless of whether the child does well in memorizing. We can guide parents in helping their children learn Scripture by providing written notes outlining ways to help that learning happen.

Possible dangers are that some parents (and even some teachers) may decide that memorization can *make* children Christians or that by the end of the sixth grade, all children should know a given set of Bible passages. Neither of these ideas is true.

Memorization programs simply undergird the involvement of our children in the life of the church. Learning Scripture passages can help children be open to the Spirit of God in their lives. Knowing the words is one thing, and it is very important; but knowing the Spirit of God in and through the words is the most important thing of all.

A Possible Memorization Plan

Because of the pitfalls associated with memorization, suggesting a specific memorization plan can be dangerous. Since knowing the language of Scripture is so important, however, the risk is one I shall take.

Many churches have developed memorization programs in recent years, most adding such programs to their regular Sunday school curriculum. I know of several in my own area and have drawn on their collective experience in compiling the suggestions that I am making here. Note that my lists of content to memorize keep in mind the differences between younger elementary children and older elementary children.

Younger Elementary (first, second, and third grades)
Matthew 6:9-13—The Lord's Prayer (in the adaptation used in your congregational worship)
Psalm 23
John 3:16

Matthew 22:37b-39—The Great Commandment
Psalm 100
Names of the books of the Bible (third grade)
Names of the disciples (third grade)

Older Elementary (fourth, fifth, and sixth grades)
Exodus 20:3-4, 7-8, 12-17—The Ten Commandments
Matthew 5:3-12—The Beatitudes
1 Corinthians 13
Romans 8:28
Psalm 121
Psalm 95:1-7

I have chosen these passages on the bases of their importance and of their continuing use by the church, not on their consistent theology or on their ritual importance to Christian belief. Many readers will wish to use a quite different list because of the individual interests of their local church or denomination.

Good memorization programs also include some liturgy, such as the Gloria Patri and the Doxology, and several key hymns in addition to portions of the Bible. We should be realistic, however, and not try to include all that we consider important. Lists that are burdensome will be a source of frustration to the children and to us as well.

WHAT MEMORIZATION DOES AND DOES NOT DO

Memorizing the names Matthew, Mark, Luke, and John does not mean that a child knows what is in those books or that a child understands them. Memorizing "God so loved the world" in John 3:16 does not mean that the child understands what those words mean or that the child believes them to be true.

Learning such information does mean that the child can draw upon memory throughout her or his life and can participate with others in doing what Christians do. The knowledge is simply part of the equipment we need to participate with others in the life of discipleship and in the church.

I am so grateful that more than fifty years ago my Sunday school teachers in Des Moines, Iowa—Edith McBeth, Mrs. Pickford, Mr. Harder, Madge Kussart, and Ethel McClellan—with good humor helped me memorize significant portions of Scripture. I have used that memory ever since. That knowledge has enabled me to feel a part of the life of the church. Whenever or wherever I entered a new church, I knew many of the words they were saying and I felt I was in "my" church.

DO WE EMPHASIZE MEANING?

At times we will lead children, especially in the first, second, and third grades, to repeat a passage of Scripture in unison and will give little emphasis to their understanding its meaning. Such will be the case with the Lord's Prayer.

Nevertheless, as teachers or parents we need to take time to answer as clearly as possible any questions the children may ask. A child may say, "My grandfather is in heaven; where is heaven?" We teachers might simply let the other children give various responses and then might say, "We don't really know where heaven is or what it is like (the truth), but Christians believe that to be in heaven is to be with God. Therefore, your grandfather is with God."

We should never hesitate to say simply, "We don't know" or "I don't know." Children understand not knowing—they do not know a lot themselves.

With fourth, fifth, and sixth graders, we will continue to say the Lord's Prayer, including it now in the worship portion of our lesson. For these children we should also build in time to talk about the meaning of words such as *heaven, hallowed,* and even *on earth.* Children's opinions, freely shared, should be welcomed without our trying to correct them. We should also send class members to a Bible dictionary to look up *heaven* and *hallow.* They will find a variety of answers for *heaven,* and they will learn that different Christians over the centuries have favored different definitions. They will often want to know "the truth," and you might say, "Well, right now, I guess I believe . . . ." Or you might say, "The church has often said that heaven is . . . ." or "In one place the Bible says that heaven is . . . ." Any of those answers will be enough because they are the truth.

POINTS TO REMEMBER

✔ Remembering the faith of the past is essential to having faith in the present.

✔ Much of the memory of the church, which we want our children to share, is found in the Bible.

✔ Children learn by hearing, by *repetition*, and by searching for meaning.

✔ Group recitation, where individual mistakes are covered up and no one looks foolish, is preferable to individual recitation unless a child is eager to speak alone.

✔ Younger elementary children often do not understand the meaning of what they are saying, but they understand that they are participating with adults in something adults consider important. That fact has meaning for them.

✔ A variety of forms of repetition—saying verses again and again in different ways, singing the verses to familiar tunes at Sunday school, saying the verses at home with a parent, hearing them read in worship—help a child learn Scripture.

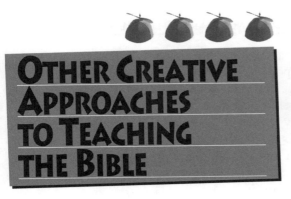

OTHER CREATIVE APPROACHES TO TEACHING THE BIBLE

STARTING WHERE CHILDREN ARE NOW

One approach to teaching the Bible to children is to begin the lesson, not with the Scripture story, but with activity or discussion drawn from children's own experiences. Starting a Bible lesson where the children are now catches their interest. Let's go back to the Lord's Prayer for an example of how this approach might work.

We start by asking these questions: Do you ever talk to anyone you love? Who are the people you like to talk to? What do you like to talk about? (We are careful to allow enough time for the children to warm up to the questions.)

We follow up with questions like these: Do you ever talk to God? What do you say to God? How do you feel when you talk to God? Why do you talk to God? What do you call what you are doing when you talk to God? (Again, we take time to allow the children to say more than simply the answers to the questions.)

Then we use these questions to bring the Scripture passage into the discussion: Do you think Jesus talked to God? What do you think Jesus talked to God about? As the children respond, we invite them to open their Bibles to Matthew 6:9-13 and to read the passage together.

We review the reading with more questions: What did Jesus say we should say to God? Do you want to talk to God right now? Who wants to start us off talking to God? All this discussion leads naturally into a time of praying the Lord's Prayer together.

PERSONAL INVOLVEMENT WITH THE STORY

Older elementary children can be both objective and subjective in the way they view life and the Bible. They can stand outside a Scripture passage and ask, "What is this passage saying? What might it have meant in Bible times?" They are also capable of moving inside a passage, putting themselves into the scene, and asking what that portion of Scripture means for them personally.

Older children can read the parable of the prodigal son and can know objectively that Jesus is saying that God is like the father: God's love is ready to forgive, and God will come to us as soon as we are ready. Boys and girls who are eleven and twelve can also realize the sins that are present in both the younger brother and the older brother and can recognize the same sins in themselves as they think and feel subjectively.

Far too often in our teaching such stories to children, we only talk *about* the parable. We do not lead our listeners into the story until it becomes their story. In order to correct this problem, we can at times let the story become *our* story. We can tell the children how the story causes *us* to be aware of our sins of selfishness and jealousy. We can tell the girls and boys how we are grateful for God's forgiveness and love in our own life. We can encourage the persons in the class to think about the story and to share their own thoughts and feelings.

To become more personal in teaching, we need to remember two things. One, this method *takes time;* and we need to take the time, not hurry. The lesson is all the things the children are learning and includes every experience during the Sunday school time. If children are interested and involved, we need to relax and feel good about what they are doing. There will be other days to cover the points in the printed lesson that we haven't gotten to yet. Two, we must be willing to share from our own life experiences. Children grow from hearing of the joys and trials of respected adults.

RESEARCH AND DISCOVERY

Research and discovery can be an exciting approach to teaching children the Bible. As we lead children in activities that allow them to research the hard questions and to explore the lives and feelings of Bible people, our learners discover more meaning in the passages. These actions are satisfying, and they build self-esteem.

To do research requires resources, but the resources do not have to be complex or expensive. Older children learn by and enjoy doing research such as interviewing persons at home, at school, and in the congregation.

Other inexpensive research can be done with resources that the church and children already have or that can be borrowed from the pastor. For example, Bible research can be done in the children's own Bibles, in other Bible translations and paraphrases available at church, in a Gospel parallel, in a Bible dictionary, in a Bible atlas, and in other Bible helps such as concordances and commentaries.

Never *tell* children to use Bible helps. *Show them how* to use various translations, Bible dictionaries, and other aids and *lead* them in using these resources. Following are Bible helps that can be used by older children and ideas about how they can be useful:

- ✔ A variety of translations and paraphrases allows children to better understand the meaning of a passage as they view that passage through the understanding of various scholars.
- ✔ A Bible dictionary contains articles on biblical events, people, groups, and ideas. It also helps with pronouncing words.
- ✔ A Bible atlas helps children identify geographic features, rivers, towns, and cities. An atlas also helps give a feeling of elevation (depth of valleys and height of hills).
- ✔ A Gospel parallel places the Gospels of Matthew, Mark, and Luke in parallel columns on the same page. This arrangement allows children to see if the same passage appears in all three Gospels, how the accounts differ, and how they are the same.

Get your church to buy one or more of each of these books. Then practice using them. If we, the teachers, are going to lead children in using these Bible helps, we must have used them ourselves.

Some of the kinds of questions that can be answered by children through research and discovery and the methods children might use in discovering the answers include the following:

- ✔ Where was Moab? Look in a Bible atlas or Bible dictionary.
- ✔ Who are the Pharisees? What did they believe? Look in a Bible dictionary.
- ✔ What are some different ways a verse has been translated or paraphrased? Look at several translations and paraphrases.
- ✔ Does the parable of the lost coin occur in Gospels other than Luke? Look in a Gospel parallel, a Bible dictionary, or a concordance.

✔ Where can I find the parable of the lost sheep? Look in a concordance or look in the Gospels in your Bible until you find it.

As we lead our boys and girls to discover information about the Bible for themselves, they will have fun and will develop skills. In the process we may find that behavior problems decline.

MUSIC AND SINGING

Over the centuries Christians have set a great deal of the Bible to music in the songs and hymns of the church. In fact, many of us learned most of what we know about the Bible from songs that have stirred our hearts with both words and music. Singing the Bible is both educational and inspirational.

Even children who think that they do not like to sing like listening to music. As they listen, they often begin humming and then singing in spite of themselves. Children sing because there is a song within them that demands expression.

Following are three statements that are good points to remember about singing the Bible with children.

1. Our children need to learn the great hymns of the church as well as the songs written for children.
2. As children sing Bible-based songs and hymns, they can be taught the Scripture that inspired the lyrics.
3. Songs and hymns, like stories, are learned by frequent repetition. If we try to use too many new songs and hymns at once, children may be unable to remember any of them.

Some short, simple songs and choruses written especially for children are useful in teaching biblical truths. However, these should never be used to the exclusion of the great hymns that also teach biblical truths in music.

When I was an elementary child, my music teacher, Miss Bell, would whisper in my ear, "Richard, I want this song to sound very good for the program, so please just whisper the words." I became known as a monotone. Since then, however, I have been told that I sing hymns quite well when I am familiar with them. By the time I get to the third or fourth stanza, I'm ready for the choir!

However well-intentioned my music teacher may have been, she was not attuned to my most important needs as a child. We must always remember that a good performance is not a fraction as important as encouraging the song in the heart of the child and the self-esteem that comes from our praise and love.

Many of us who teach are not musically inclined. We feel inadequate in using music with children. Not every classroom has a piano or a person to play it either. Nevertheless, sing-along audiotapes and CD's are usually available for purchase as part of children's curriculum. These resources help children learn biblical truths, and we should use these resources as much as possible.

PICTURES, ART, AND GRAPHICS

During the Middle Ages, when few people had access to the Bible, children and adults alike became more knowledgeable of the Christian faith and of the Bible by observing the beautiful stained-glass windows of the churches and cathedrals.

Those of us who attend churches with biblical-art windows can use them for teaching elementary children. We can take groups of children to stand in front of the windows and can lead the children in talking about the Bible stories. Or if our church has biblical pictures on walls throughout the building, we can send elementary children on a scavenger hunt to match Scripture passages to art.

Often pictures that come in our Sunday school resources and pictures that are found in books of great masterpieces are based on biblical themes and stories and can be useful in teaching the themes and stories to children. Some churches have closets or resource rooms where such pictures are stored after their first use. Most churches have not kept up with these pictures, however, and cannot find them when they are needed.

An important resource for any church to have is a picture file in which pictures of various sizes can be kept. If the pictures can be indexed by subject, they will be used more frequently.

A major function of paintings is to stimulate the imagination. As the artist has used her or his imagination to construct the painting, so we need to use our imagination when we view and interpret what we see. Children can be led to wonder and think about the picture they are viewing. This activity can stimulate children to see new possibilities in the biblical story.

We need to stress to our children that we do not really know what any biblical person looked like, however. In our time, children tend to believe what they see. We need to help them realize that what they are looking at is only a representation of that figure by that artist. We can point out that biblical pictures usually reflect the culture and the historical period in which they were painted. Understanding the differences allows children to realize that people view Jesus and other persons in the Bible through their own perception and time. Even so, such art is valuable in helping children get into and understand the Bible.

POINTS TO REMEMBER

✔ Children are helped to own Bible stories when they are encouraged to talk about their thoughts and feelings.

✔ Questions that allow children to do more than simply give an answer can help them imagine the world of the Bible.

✔ Children learn best when they discover answers by themselves.

✔ Children sing because there is a song within them that demands expression.

✔ Art stimulates the imagination, both in the artist and in the observer.

LEARNING TO TEACH BY SHARING AND PRACTICE

WHAT IS A SHARING AND PRACTICE SESSION?

All of us who teach elementary children want to help children grow in the Christian faith and in the knowledge and love of the Bible. Some of us are inexperienced and know little about the Bible. Most of us are devoted to our jobs and careers throughout the week and are busy at home as well. Nevertheless, regardless of our situation, experience, shape, size, age, or gender, God can use us in the teaching ministry.

In *Living and Learning in the Church School*, Phoebe M. Anderson says, "A church school teacher's chief function is neither to dispense information nor to declare the moral law. It is to love God's children, young and old" (United Church Press, 1965; page 87). The Holy Spirit can enable most of us to both love and help elementary children. Sharing and practice sessions are one way we can cooperate with the Spirit in helping one another. They are opportunities for us to *support* and *enable* one another in the art of teaching.

Good sharing and practice sessions have these features:

✔ Meetings are scheduled for the convenience of those attending and last about an hour and a half.

✔ Meetings start and end on time.

✔ Childcare is offered for those teachers who would not otherwise be able to attend.

✔ Each session focuses on *one* skill.

✔ Sessions include teachers of both younger elementary and older elementary children (and may be open to preschool teachers).

✔ Over the course of several sessions, teachers have opportunities to practice a variety of skills and to share their insights and approaches.

Let's look at some possible sharing and practice exercises for teaching methods discussed in previous chapters.

TELLING BIBLE STORIES

One of the best ways to improve as a teller of Bible stories is to share and practice with others who are engaged in the same process. In order to get the most out of such a session, I suggest the following plan.

Let everyone choose a partner. Then give partners a few minutes to begin to feel comfortable with each other. The ability to relax is important at this point. A helpful opening exercise is to have everyone tell his or her partner about one childhood Sunday school experience she or he remembers.

Use the story of the prodigal son (Luke 15:11-32) as the Bible story for partners to practice telling. Ask each pair to follow these steps:

1. First, read through the story individually.
2. Pray together that God's Spirit will stir imagination and bring insight.
3. Individually write down your key observations *about* the story. Different individuals may notice different things:

   ✔ Jesus is telling a parable about God.
   ✔ Both the younger son and the older son are realistic persons with whom we can identify.
   ✔ The father (like most of us) is often puzzled concerning his sons. He does not really understand them, but he always loves them.
   ✔ The father is anxious to restore and reconcile.

4. Share with each other what you have noted about the story.
5. Now focus on the learners. Discuss how children will hear or understand this story if we retell it to them. Begin by focusing on the learning abilities of younger elementary children. Can younger elementary children really think of the father in the story as God? Probably not. For them, he is simply a father. What about older elementary children? What difference will their beginning ability to think symbolically make in the way we can tell and share the story?

6. Individually prepare your own version of the story as you would tell it to younger elementary children.

7. Relax and share the stories with each other. Listen carefully to each other, praising the best parts in each story and noticing where the storytelling touches emotions. Is there excitement? When? Is there suspense? Where?

8. After this first set of stories, individually think about the story you told and make some notes about how you would improve the telling of the story.

9. Move to a second round of practice, this time focused on older elementary children. How should the telling change? Can different kinds of questions be asked? Can you share with older elementary children examples of your own experience in response to the story?

Using this approach, partners will build important insights— not only into the Bible stories and into the art of storytelling, but also into the ways children hear and participate.

ENCOURAGING PERSONAL INVOLVEMENT

Chapter 4 discusses older children's ability to become personally involved in Bible stories. But how do teachers themselves get involved? Try this:

1. Form your group of teachers into a circle and discuss among yourselves ideas for leading children in playing out a story. Work with the story of Jesus healing the paralytic lowered through the roof by four friends. Listen to one another's ideas. Then let each teacher decide which role she or he will assume in the story. Will you be one of the friends, one of the crowd, or the paralytic? How do you feel? Why did you choose that role?

2. Practice the roles. Play out little skits of the story and talk about how younger and older elementary children would react.

3. Discuss ways to involve your children emotionally as well as with understanding. Share how you as teachers are feeling.

4. Practice other stories and plan how you will involve the children emotionally in the stories you have selected.

MEMORIZING BY AND FOR PARTICIPATION

Lead a discussion of the guidelines for memorization suggested in Chapter 3. What comments and suggestions do the teachers have? Then follow this plan:

1. Ask teachers to identify one way of memorizing that would appeal to the children in their class.
2. Say the Lord's Prayer in unison. Share feelings about praying in unison.
3. Can teachers recall when and how they first learned the prayer? Talk in pairs about those memories, then pray the prayer again.
4. Find out how many of the suggested passages for memorization your group knows.
5. Choose one that most of you do not remember. Practice quietly by yourselves on the first three verses. Then say the first verse in unison as a group. Say all of the verses in unison three times.
6. Divide into pairs and say the verses to each other. Smile a lot. Laugh a little. Have a good time. Learn, share, and practice.

USING BIBLE HELPS WITH OLDER CHILDREN

Working in groups of two or three people, use the following suggestions for sharing and practice in using Bible helps:

1. Use a Bible dictionary to look for information on the Pharisees. You will probably find an article several pages long. Look up several other words or people who have appeared in your Sunday school material lately.
2. Now practice using a Bible atlas. Where did the Exodus take place? When did it happen? During Jesus' life what did the Holy Land look like? Where was the Jordan River? the Sea of Galilee?
3. Practice using a Gospel parallel. Look up Matthew 13, the parable of the sower. Does it appear in other Gospels? How do the passages differ?
4. Gather two or three translations of the Bible, including a paraphrase, and compare various portions of the Bible in each. Discuss how you might use these with older children.

Many teachers say they didn't *really* learn much in Sunday school until they began to teach. Sharing and practice strengthen that learning process.

Finally, if you have the opportunity, join a Bible study group or find another Sunday school teacher who will partner with you for Bible study. Covenant together to read the Bible passages for the Sunday school lesson by Thursday of each week, then to discuss the passages together either in a face-to-face meeting or by telephone. Plan to share ideas for teaching the passage and to pray together.

POINTS TO REMEMBER

✔ Whether we have taught for only a short time or have years of teaching experience, we can continue to learn ways to help children grow in the Christian faith.

✔ Sharing and Practice sessions help teachers to be better teachers of elementary children.

✔ Humor and relaxation help in learning.

✔ One of the major rewards of teaching is learning.

6 PRESENTING BIBLES TO CHILDREN

By Ruth Murray Alexander

Like many other adults, my father, Dick Murray, still has the Bible that was given to him by his home church in 1934. He no longer uses that Bible. In fact, the pages are yellow, and the print is too small for him to read. He says that for the first several months after receiving that Bible, he took pride in reading parts of it and in keeping it by his bed. That Bible was the first adult book that was really his.

As the Christian community, part of the Body of Christ, it is our responsibility to pass along our tools of the faith to the next generation. Our primary tangible tool is the Bible itself. Most churches present Bibles to children at a designated age (that varies from church to church). Many churches decide to present Bibles to children who are entering the third or fourth grade.

Churches might consider giving Bibles to children at least twice during their growing-up years. The child's reading level, the translation most used by a church, and the ways in which the Bible will be used by the child all change. These factors can help determine the times for presentation and the types of Bible presented.

As the membership of your church changes, so will the children of your church. Individual Bible presentations may need to be made from time to time as new children move into your church.

THE SETTING

The setting for the presentation of Bibles can vary not only from church to church but from year to year within the same church. Tradition holds a lot of weight with most congregations, but it is sometimes helpful to be bold and to try new ideas. The suggestions in this chapter are intended to help you create a setting that meets your needs. You will have ideas of your own, and you will want to choose the type of event that matches your children and your church. The most important consideration is to make the event special and unforgettable. Children love ceremony, and even the simplest service can be meaningful and memorable to a child.

A pastor's visit to the children's Sunday school class in preparation for the event can help build excitement. The pastor can talk about the history of the Bible, the way that the Scriptures are used in worship, and the importance of the stories that have been passed down for thousands of years. Children can understand that the Bible tells us about the nature of God and about how God has been revealed to people.

Having the child's name clearly printed on the cover or written in calligraphy on a presentation page in the Bible is important. It is also helpful to have as many ministerial and lay representatives' signatures on the presentation page as possible. List the names of children receiving Bibles in the bulletin and in your church newsletter.

THE SERVICE

Bible presentations are best done as part of a worship service with the congregation present. In that way children can experience the affirmation of the entire church as the congregation gives them their Bibles.

Encourage parents to attend the presentation and to stand behind their children at the altar. The presentation itself should involve the congregation; lay representatives, such as the Sunday school superintendent, the children's coordinator, and/or the children's Sunday school teacher(s); the church staff; the children receiving Bibles; and their families. If possible, also include close family friends. In this way the children are surrounded by the entire congregation.

The entire worship service may center on the Bible and its place in our lives. Older children may lead the congregational Scripture reading, and all children can have a special place in the service.

Following are three litanies for possible use in your service. In every case the child's full name is to be called out to the congregation as each Bible is presented.

(Discipleship Resources grants permission to reproduce these litanies in quantity for use in your congregation.)

PRESENTATION OF BIBLES

LITANY 1

Sunday School Superintendent: Christians are a people of the Book. That book, the Bible, is the church's book. The church chose what to include, how to arrange the parts, and what to leave out. We—you and I—are the church. The Bible, the church's book, is our book.

The Bible is our book because of what we believe this book reveals—a living God whom we know in Jesus Christ. We believe that Jesus Christ is the living Word of God, and we must know the Bible if we are to know Jesus Christ.

Teacher, Children's Coordinator, or Superintendent: The members of our church are pleased to present you, our children, with these Bibles. We acknowledge you as important members of our community and congregation. It is our hope that you will use your Bible regularly and that you will ask questions and seek help until you find answers and understanding.

Congregation: As Christians we are charged with the responsibility of sharing the Christian faith through Scripture, reason, tradition, and experience. May God help us do so with wisdom, love, mutual respect, and understanding.

All: AMEN.

LITANY 2

Pastor: O living God, made known to us in the Bible, we have named these children as your servants and into their hands we place your Word.

Congregation: Recognizing these children as growing members of our faith community, we pray that as the Word is placed into their hands, so it will be written upon their hearts.

Pastor: Children, will you accept the Holy Bible as the truth of God, and will you carry it with faith into your generation?

Children: We will, with God's help.

LITANY 3

Pastor: Today we celebrate a special event: the presentation of Bibles to you, our third graders. The Bible is a special book because it contains the story of God and of persons who lived and followed God. We as the church believe that this story is an important one for you to hear and to experience.

Children: We are eager to begin our adventure with our Bibles, but we will need your help. We will have many questions.

Pastor: Parents and sponsors, will you assist these children in your homes—guiding them as they study, sharing your understanding of the story of faith, and giving them the opportunity to benefit together in Christian education programs?

Parents and Sponsors: Yes. We take seriously our responsibility for helping our children as they encounter the Bible. With God's guidance, we will lead them, share with them, and provide them with learning experiences and fellowship.

Congregation: As a congregation, we too have the privilege and responsibility to share our faith stories and to support these young people as they learn and grow. We pray for God's guidance and grace in this endeavor.

All: Loving God, we give thanks for the Bible, your gift to be used for our learning. Help us to hear its words, to understand them, and to be changed by them so that in your time we may become wiser, more loving, and more active Christians. In the name of Christ we pray. Amen.

OTHER IDEAS FOR PRESENTATION

Another time and arena in which Bibles can be presented is during the Sunday school hour, with parents invited to be present. After the presentation, parents and children can be led through an exercise in Bible discovery. The leader can hold up familiar verses, and children and adults can try to find the verses together. Special bookmarks can be made, and refreshments can be served.

Sometimes Bibles are presented by an adult class who wish to sponsor the event. In fact, individual adults may wish to serve as Bible partners, coming into class from time to time to support the children in Bible study. This assistance can be helpful because younger elementary children may experience initial difficulty while exploring the Bible.

Many times adults have said, "I still have that Bible that was given to me by my church when I was a child; it means a lot to me." Whenever we hear this or similar statements, we know that the Christian faith is being passed to the next generation through the church's book—the Bible.

GUIDELINES FOR PRESENTING BIBLES

✔ Every church, even those with only one or two children, should give Bibles to the girls and boys in the third or fourth grade.

✔ Giving the Bibles should take place in a special presentation during a worship service or at some other time anticipated and planned for.

✔ The pastor, parents, teachers, and other church officers should be involved in the presentation.

✔ The church should give the Bible translation most used in that church's curriculum resources. For most churches, this version is the New Revised Standard Version or the New International Version. Some churches may prefer to give the American Bible Society's Contemporary English Version or the *Good News Bible: The Bible in Today's English Version*.

✔ The entire church should continue to work with children to help make the God of the Bible alive and real for them.

✔ Each child should be enabled to think and feel, *This is my Bible. My church gave it to me.*

A WORD FROM THE AUTHOR

As a child at First United Methodist Church in Des Moines, Iowa, I had a Sunday school perfect-attendance pin that was so long I could have tripped on it. My memories of those years in Sunday school focus on the persons who were my teachers. I have named several of them in the dedication; other names that should be there have faded from my memory after so many years. These teachers knew me, loved me, and led me to want to share the Christian faith that they so obviously cherished.

THE BIBLE IN MY CHILDHOOD

In the nursery Edith McBeth held me, rocked me, and told me about the baby Jesus. She did the same for countless others over a period of more than sixty years. Jeanette Pickford told and retold many of the stories of the Bible and helped me begin to use the Bible for myself. Madge Kussart led the older children in enjoying memorizing John 3:16. I will never forget her enthusiasm and her sense of fun. Mr. Harder, a quiet man who was a lawyer, had me make lists in a notebook of the positive characteristics of the heroes of the Old Testament. (He also started me collecting stamps, a hobby I continue to enjoy.)

When I was twelve, I joined the church and signed my name in the same membership book that my mother had signed as a girl many years previously. I knew that I was a part of a loving portion of God's holy church. And as a result of my teachers' efforts up to that time, the Bible seemed to me to be my book, even though I knew only brief portions of it.

Later, during my years as a professor of Christian education, I became aware that teaching the Bible to children had gone through, and was continuing to experience, a variety of changes in development and that some stages of its history were quite different from what I experienced as a child.

TEACHING THE BIBLE TO CHILDREN— A HISTORICAL REFLECTION

Sometime shortly after my birth, a study was made of the relationship between biblical knowledge and honesty in twelve-year-old boys. Boys in Sunday schools, parochial schools, public schools, and reform schools were tested. The test results produced no evidence of a relationship between biblical knowledge and honesty in the boys tested. Some boys who could quote many Bible verses were found to be dishonest. Other boys who knew few if any portions of the Bible were quite honest.

Those results were shocking to many. At that time many church educators firmly believed that memorizing Bible verses would make girls and boys more Christian and would certainly help them be honest. Those educators wondered what had gone wrong.

At the same time, under the influence of persons like John Dewey, a prominent educator-philosopher of the day, people were discovering the importance of the individual child and how each learned and changed. Emphasis shifted from teaching to learning and from content—for example, the biblical lesson—to the learning child. New emphasis on the child as a child rather than as a little adult and careful study of the nature of childhood moved Christian education forward.

These new perspectives, however, created confusion about the role of the Bible in Christian teaching. The Bible was often referred to as a resource to draw upon for special emphasis rather than as the major book that all children should learn as Christians.

Thus during the 1950's and 1960's many of us did not stress the use of the Bible in teaching children. Instead teachers used contemporary stories to stress moral values such as kindness and honesty. Teaching emphasis was put on life experiences with which children could easily relate. Denominational curriculum deliberately contained few printed Bible passages. Only biblical references were given. The idea behind not printing the passages was that both teachers and children would be forced to use the Bible itself to look up the references given. Unfortunately, this practice simply resulted in less use of the Bible, although we could always point to references to quotations and biblical stories in every Sunday's lesson. Many of today's parents of young children were raised during this era. Now they feel ignorant of the basic biblical stories.

During the 1970's, under pressure from a variety of sources, including the more conservative elements of our churches, denominational curriculum began to put more emphasis on the Bible itself. From that time throughout the 1980's and 1990's, biblical stories and passages have been central to printed lessons for children. Sometimes as parents, teachers, and church leaders, we have confused quantity with quality, however. Stress on learning an *abundance* of Bible verses may not be the best use of the Bible in the Christian education of elementary children.

All these shifts have occurred during the seventy-three years of my life, and I have taken part in each. Today we look for clues to a quality relationship between our children and the Bible. Our goal in Christian education is that children will become increasingly aware of God's seeking love as known especially in Jesus Christ.

This awareness of God's love comes from our children's relationships with parents, with their larger family, and with the entire church of which they are a part. However, the center of that awareness of God's love comes from repeated exposure to the biblical message of God's continual seeking of the early Hebrews and the Christian church. Through story after story in the Bible, God seeks and men and women turn away. But God keeps on seeking and finally enters into human history in Jesus Christ.

As they develop an increasing awareness of God's seeking love, we believe that our children will respond in faith and love. They will become disciples of Jesus Christ who serve God and God's people.

FOR FURTHER READING

Adventures With the Bible: A Sourcebook for Teachers of Children, by Dorothy Jean Furnish (Abingdon Press, 1995)

The Bible in Christian Education, by Iris V. Cully (Augsburg, 1995)

Children Worship! by MaryJane Pierce Norton (Discipleship Resources, 1997)

Experiencing the Bible With Children, by Dorothy Jean Furnish (Abingdon Press, 1990).

Foundations: Shaping the Ministry of Christian Education in Your Congregation (Discipleship Resources, 1993)

Helping Children Feel at Home in Church, by Margie Morris (Discipleship Resources, revised 1997)

How Do Our Children Grow? by Delia Touchton Halverson (Abingdon Press, 1993)

New Ways to Tell the Old, Old Story: Choosing and Using Bible Stories With Children and Youth, by Delia Touchton Halverson (Abingdon Press, 1992)

Planning for Christian Education: A Practical Guide for Your Congregation, edited by Carol F. Krau (Discipleship Resources, 1994)

Resources for Use With Elementary Children

Bible Teaching Pictures (Abingdon Press)

Set   1: *Moses, the Exodus, and the Promised Land* (1996)
Set   2: *Favorite Old Testament Stories* (1997)
Set   3: *The Patriarchs: Abraham to Joseph* (1997)
Set   4: *The Prophets, the Exile, and the Return* (1998)
Set   5: *Samuel, Saul, and David* (1998)
Set   6: *Creation* (1999)
Set   7: *Jesus Is Born* (1996)
Set   8: *Lent and Easter* (1997)
Set   9: *Stories About Jesus* (1997)
Set 10: *Pentecost and the Early Church* (1998)
Set 11: *Parables of Jesus* (1998)
Set 12: *Heroes and Heroines of the Early Church* (1999)

Bible Zone: Where the Bible Comes to Life—Younger Elementary FunAction Experience Kit, by LeeDell Stickler (Abingdon Press, 1997); *Older Elementary FunAction Experience Kit,* by Judy Newman-St.John (Abingdon Press, 1997)

Don't Just Sit There: Bible Stories That Move You, for Ages 6–8, by LeeDell Stickler (Abingdon Press, 1997)

FaithHome (studies for family settings), by Debra Ball-Kilbourne and MaryJane Pierce Norton; created by Bishop Dan Solomon and Joy Solomon (Abingdon Press, 1997)

Finding Your Way Through the Bible: Revised NRSV Edition, by Carolyn and Paul Maves (Abingdon Press, 1992)

Forbid Them Not: Involving Children in Sunday Worship, Years A, B, and C, by Carolyn C. Brown (three volumes supporting the Revised Common Lectionary; Abingdon Press, 1992, 1993, 1994)